Texas
The Lone Star State

Tika Downey

PowerKiDS press™

New York

Published in 2010 by The Rosen Publishing Group, Inc.
29 East 21st Street, New York, NY 10010

First Edition

Editor: Joanne Randolph
Book Design: Greg Tucker
Photo Researcher: Jessica Gerweck

Photo Credits: Cover Ian Shive/Getty Images; p. 5 Nicolas Russell/Getty Images; pp. 7, 22 (famous people) Getty Images; p. 9 © Randy Faris/Corbis; pp. 11, 15, 19, 22 (animal), 22 (bird), 22 (flower) Shutterstock.com; p. 13 © Eric and David Hosking/Corbis; p. 17 © Richard Cummins/Corbis; p. 22 (tree) © www.istockphoto.com/Kathy Hicks.

Library of Congress Cataloging-in-Publication Data

Downey, Tika.
  Texas : the Lone Star State / Tika Downey. — 1st ed.
     p. cm. — (Our amazing states)
  Includes bibliographical references and index.
  ISBN 978-1-4042-8112-7 (library binding) — ISBN 978-1-4358-3344-9 (pbk.) — ISBN 978-1-4358-3345-6 (6-pack)
  1. Texas—Juvenile literature. I. Title.
  F386.3.D69 2010
  976.4—dc22

                              2009000542

Manufactured in the United States of America

Contents

The Lone Star State

Do you imagine cowboys, herds of cows, and wide, open spaces when you think of Texas? Many people do. Texas has all those things, plus oil fields, big cities, and the Lyndon B. Johnson Space Center.

Texas is in the southern United States, just north of Mexico. In fact, Texas once belonged to Mexico. Then it became a free country called the **Republic** of Texas. The republic's flag had one star, which stood for Texas as an **independent** nation. Texas kept the flag as its state flag when it became part of the United States. That is why it is called the Lone Star State.

Here two ranchers herd some cattle. Raising cattle has been a major business in Texas for over 300 years.

Texas's Past

People have lived in Texas for about 37,000 years! That is when the earliest Native Americans arrived. Then, in 1519, Spanish **explorers** claimed the land for Spain. Spanish settlers began to arrive in 1690. Mexico took control of Texas after becoming independent from Spain in 1821. Settlers from the United States started arriving that same year.

Texan settlers grew unhappy with Mexican rule and won a war for independence in 1836. Texas was its own republic until 1845, when it became the twenty-eighth state.

Cowboys, farmers, and railroads helped Texas grow. The discovery of oil in 1866 also helped many Texans become rich.

These workers are drilling for oil at Spindletop Hill, in Beaumont, Texas. Spindletop is where the first large oil field was discovered in Texas in 1901.

Remember the Alamo!

Have you heard of the Alamo? It is in San Antonio and is one of the most famous places in Texas. It was built as a Spanish **mission** in 1718. It became famous because of the battle that was fought there in 1836.

The Battle of the Alamo happened during Texas's war for independence. Thousands of Mexican soldiers attacked Texan fighters inside the Alamo. There were fewer than 200 Texan fighters. They could not win, but they fought bravely until the end.

The fighters' bravery **inspired** the people of Texas. "Remember the Alamo!" became a battle cry to remind them why they were fighting for independence.

About 2.5 million people visit the Alamo each year. The Texan fighters held their ground against the Mexicans for 13 days inside the building shown here.

Lone Star Land and Weather

Texas is huge. This means it has many types of land and weather. Texas has lowlands, hilly plains, mountains, and valleys. Its largest river is the Rio Grande, which forms the state's border with Mexico. The Guadalupe Mountains in the west have Guadalupe **Peak**, the state's highest point, and McKittrick **Canyon**. El Capitan is another high peak in the Guadalupe Mountains.

East Texas is rainy, but the west is dry. Most of Texas is warm. The Rio Grande valley has the warmest weather. The coldest weather is in the panhandle, which is the piece of land that sticks up in the north.

El Capitan, shown here, rises 2,400 feet (731.5 m) above Pine Springs and is 8,085 feet (2,464 m) above sea level. Its name means "the captain" in Spanish.

Wild Texas

Texas's many kinds of land and weather allow many sorts of plants and animals to live there. It has cacti, forests, more than 500 types of grasses, and more than 4,000 kinds of wildflowers! Alligators, buffaloes, turkeys, and wild pigs all live in Texas, too.

One strange Texan animal is the armadillo. It is a **mammal** with a shell! Bony plates just under the skin keep it safe from enemies. The armadillo is one of Texas's official state animals.

The Texas horned lizard is the state **reptile**. Horns on its head and the sides of its body keep it safe from enemies. If the horned lizard gets really scared, it can shoot blood from its eyes!

The nine-banded armadillo, shown here, was picked as Texas's official small mammal in 1995. Armadillos dig in the ground to find food, such as bugs and small animals.

Texas Trade

For many people, Texas means oil. There is a reason for that. Texas produces more oil and natural gas than any other state. Texas also has factories that make everything from clothes to machines for oil companies.

Farming is also important. Farms and **ranches** cover about three-fourths of Texas. Ranches raise cattle for meat. Farms raise chicken, sheep, and hogs and grow cotton, corn, wheat, rice, and peanuts. You may think of Florida when you think of oranges. In fact, many of the nation's oranges come from Texan farms in the Rio Grande valley. Most of the soft, silky **mohair** produced in the United States comes from Angora goats raised in Texas!

This is an oil pump jack on the Texas panhandle. Pump jacks are used to pull oil from the ground.

Austin Is Awesome

   Austin, the Texas capital, was founded in 1839. It became the capital of the Republic of Texas in 1840. The state capitol building was built in 1888 out of pink stone, called sunset red granite. It is set on Austin's highest point.

   Austin is famous for its parks. It is also famous as a music center. You can hear bands play all kinds of music there. Austin also has **recording studios**. Many movies are made in and around Austin, too.

   Would you believe that Austin is also famous for its bats? Hundreds of thousands of bats live under the Congress Avenue Bridge. People like to gather in the evening to watch them fly out to hunt bugs!

Here you can see Texas's capitol building at sunset. In 1993, for more stories were added to the capitol, all of them underground!

Big Bend

Way out in western Texas, where the Rio Grande makes a sharp turn, is a wild place called Big Bend National Park. In the park, you can see deserts, deep canyons, and mountains that are 60 million years old! There are **fossil** trees millions of years old and caves where people lived thousands of years ago.

Big Bend is famous for its many kinds of cacti, birds, and bats. It also has willow, oak, and pine trees. You can see coyotes, mountain lions, rattlesnakes, and beavers in the park, too! Big Bend is one of the last great wild places in Texas. Big Bend also has more dinosaur fossils than any other national park. The remains of more than 90 kinds of dinosaurs have been found there.

Hundreds of millions of years ago, Big Bend used to be covered by the ocean. Today it is mostly desert, though a large number of plants and animals live along the Rio Grande.

A Traveler's Guide to Texas

Texans are proud to share their land and history with visitors. At Palo Duro Canyon State Park, you can see colorful rocks and fossils. There are also paintings, tools, and other objects made by people who lived thousands of years ago. Dinosaur Valley State Park has footprints left by dinosaurs 100 million years ago!

King Ranch, the nation's largest ranch, is a great place to see a working ranch and to learn about ranching history. You could visit Dallas, Austin, Houston, or one of Texas's other cities. You can go to museums and swim at beaches, too. What would you like to do in Texas?

Glossary

canyon (KAN-yun) A deep, sometimes narrow valley.

explorers (ek-SPLOR-urz) People who travel and look for new land.

fossil (FAH-sul) The hardened remains of a dead animal or plant.

independent (in-dih-PEN-dent) Free from the control of others.

inspired (in-SPY-urd) Moved someone to do something.

mammal (MA-mul) A warm-blooded animal that has a backbone and hair, breathes air, and feeds milk to its young.

mission (MIH-shun) A place where church leaders teach their beliefs and help the community.

mohair (MOH-hehr) Yarn or cloth made from the long, silky hair of Angora goats.

peak (PEEK) The very top of something.

ranches (RAN-chiz) Large farms for raising cattle, horses, or sheep.

recording studios (rih-KOHR-ding STOO-dee-ohz) Places where musicians record their music.

reptile (REP-tyl) A cold-blooded animal with lungs and scales.

republic (rih-PUH-blik) A form of government in which the people elect representatives who run the government.

Texas State Symbols

State Tree
Pecan

State Animal
Texas Longhorn

State Flag

State Bird
Mockingbird

State Flower
Bluebonnet

State Seal

Famous People from Texas

Stephen F. Austin
(1793–1836)
Born in Virginia
(moved to Texas 1821)
Father of Texas

Dwight Eisenhower
(1890–1969)
Born in Denison, TX
U.S. President

Lance Armstrong
(1971–)
Born in Plano, TX
Professional Racing
Cyclist

Texas State Map

Amarillo

Lubbock

Wichita Falls

Red River

Lake Texarkana

Abilene

Dallas

Ft. Worth

Sabine River

Lake Whitney

Guadalupe Mountains

El Paso

Colorado River

Brazos River

Galveston

Austin

Houston

Sabine Lake

Rio Grande

San Antonio

Corpus Christi

Laredo

Legend

○ Major City

✪ Capital

～ River

Texas State Facts

Population: About 23,904,380

Area: About 266,807 square miles (691,027 sq km)

Motto: "Friendship"

Song: "Texas, Our Texas" by William J. Marsh

Index

Web Sites

Due to the changing nature of Internet links, PowerKids Press has developed an online list of Web sites related to the subject of this book. This site is updated regularly. Please use this link to access the list:

www.powerkidslinks.com/amst/tx/